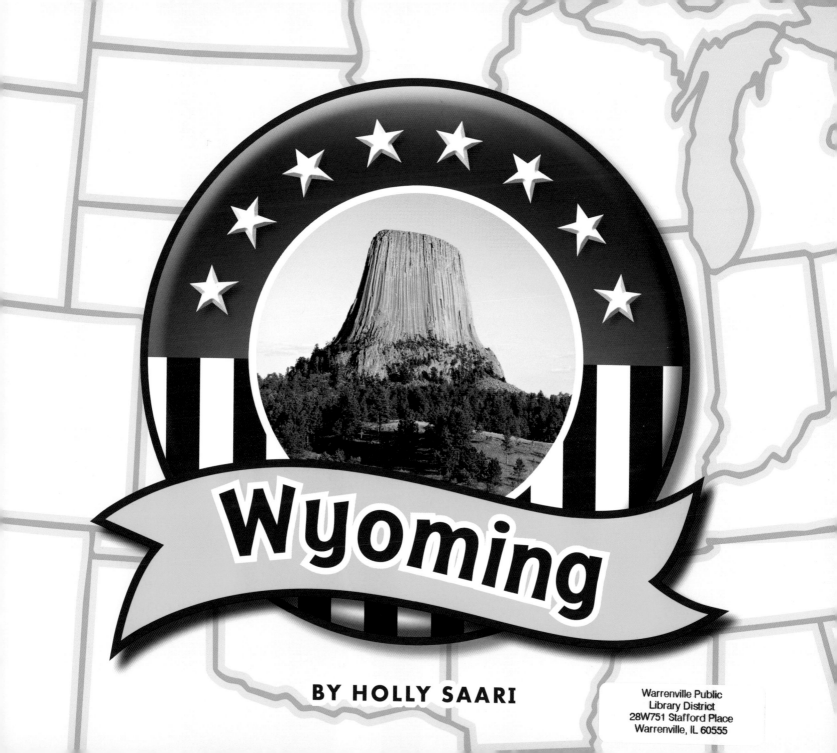

Wyoming

BY HOLLY SAARI

The Child's World

Published by The Child's World®
1980 Lookout Drive • Mankato, MN 56003-1705
800-599-READ • www.childsworld.com

ACKNOWLEDGMENTS
The Child's World®: Mary Berendes, Publishing Director
The Design Lab: Design and production
Red Line Editorial: Editorial direction

PHOTO CREDITS: Sascha Burkard/Shutterstock Images, cover, 1, 3; Matt Kania/Map Hero, Inc., 4, 5; Chuck Pefley/Photolibrary, 7; Aimin Tang/iStockphoto, 9; iStockphoto, 10; Angela Cable/iStockphoto, 11; Sascha Burkard/Bigstock, 13; North Wind Picture Archives/Photolibrary, 15; Bradley L Marlow/iStockphoto, 17; Ron Edmonds/AP Images, 19; LindyCro/Shutterstock Images, 21; One Mile Up, 22; Quarter-dollar coin image from the United States Mint, 22

LIBRARY OF CONGRESS CATALOGING-IN-PUBLICATION DATA
Saari, Holly.
  Wyoming / by Holly Saari.
     p. cm.
  Includes bibliographical references and index.
  ISBN 978-1-60253-496-4 (library bound : alk. paper)
  1. Wyoming—Juvenile literature. I. Title.
  F761.3.S23 2010
  978.7—dc22

                              2010019927

Printed in the United States of America in Mankato, Minnesota.
July 2010
F11538

On the cover:
Devils Tower became the first national **monument** in 1906.

CONTENTS

Geography

Let's explore Wyoming! Wyoming is in the western United States.

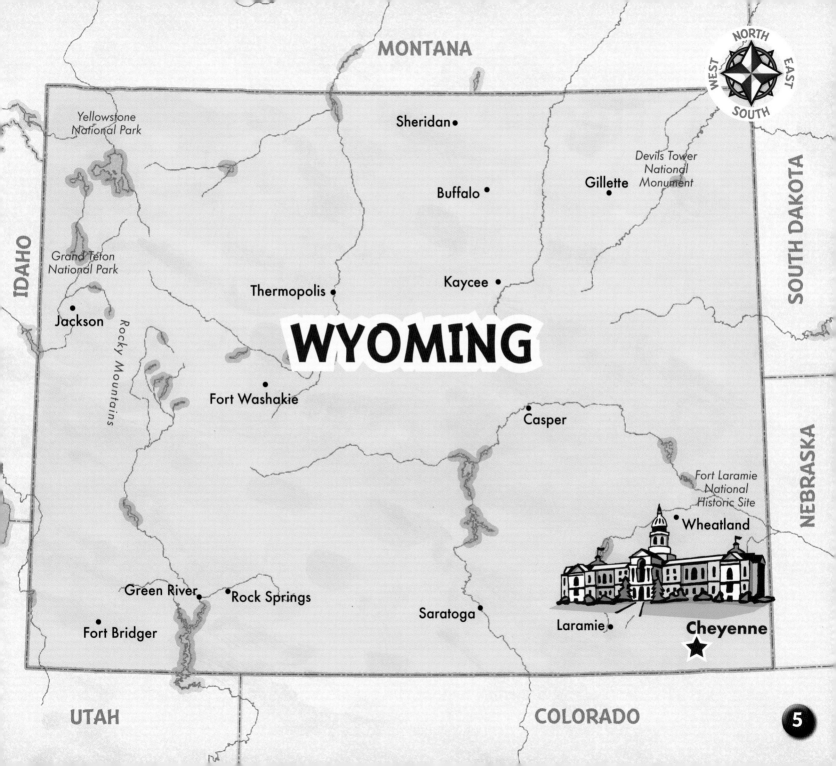

MONTANA

NORTH
WEST EAST
SOUTH

IDAHO

Yellowstone
National Park

Sheridan•

Devils Tower
National
Monument

Buffalo•

Gillette•

Grand Teton
National Park

Kaycee•

•Jackson

Thermopolis•

WYOMING

Rocky Mountains

Fort Washakie•

•Casper

Fort Laramie
National
Historic Site

•Wheatland

Green River•

•Rock Springs

•Saratoga

•Fort Bridger

Laramie•

Cheyenne
★

SOUTH DAKOTA

NEBRASKA

UTAH

COLORADO

Cities

Cheyenne is the capital of Wyoming. It is also the largest city. Casper is the second-largest city.

Casper is home to more than 50,000 people. ▶

Land

Wyoming is known for its many mountains. The Rocky Mountains run through the state. This is the biggest mountain range in North America. Wyoming also has flat, grassy areas called **plains**. There are many rivers in the state.

The Continental Divide cuts through Wyoming. Water to the east of the Divide flows toward the Atlantic Ocean. Water to the west of the Divide flows toward the Pacific Ocean.

Grand Teton National Park has beautiful, rugged mountains. ▶

Plants and Animals

Many plants and animals are found in Wyoming. The state flower is the Indian paintbrush. It has small red **petals**. The state **mammal** is the bison. This is a large, brown animal with horns. The state bird is the meadowlark.

The Indian paintbrush became Wyoming's state flower in 1917. ▶

People and Work

Of all the 50 states, Wyoming has the fewest people living in it. It has about 530,000 people. Some people work in the government or in **tourism**. Some people cut down trees or mine for coal or oil. Natural gas is an important product. Others raise animals such as cattle on **ranches**.

Some large U.S. cities have more people than all of Wyoming.

Some Wyoming farmers grow hay, sugar beets, or wheat. ▶

History

Native Americans have lived in the Wyoming area for thousands of years. In the 1800s, people from Europe came to live in the area. They trapped animals for their fur. Then more people came through on their way west. On July 10, 1890, Wyoming became the forty-fourth state.

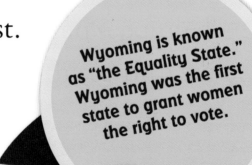

Wyoming is known as "the Equality State." Wyoming was the first state to grant women the right to vote.

Fort Laramie was a trading post and **military** fort in eastern Wyoming. ▶

Ways of Life

Wyoming has many things to do. **Museums** show items from the state's history. In the winter, people like to ski in the mountains. Hunting and fishing are **popular**, too. Some visit the national parks. Many people explore the forests or go camping.

Skiing is a popular activity in Wyoming. ▶

Famous People

Dick Cheney is a former vice president of the United States. He grew up in Wyoming. "Buffalo Bill" Cody spent time in Wyoming later in his life. He created a traveling show that displayed what life was like in the West. Jackson Pollock was a famous artist. He was born in Wyoming.

Dick Cheney was vice president of the United States from 2001 to 2009. ▶

Famous Places

Devils Tower is in northeastern Wyoming. It is a large rock. It rises more than 1,200 feet (366 m) in the air. Yellowstone National Park is a popular place to visit. It was the first national park in the country. It has many **geysers**. These are places where hot water sprays up through holes in the ground.

Old Faithful is a famous geyser in Yellowstone National Park. ▶

State Symbols

Seal

A woman on Wyoming's seal stands for Wyoming being an equal rights state. Go to childsworld.com/links for a link to Wyoming's state Web site, where you can get a firsthand look at the state seal.

Flag

Wyoming's flag has the same colors as the United States flag. It also has a bison, the state mammal.

Quarter

A **cowboy** and horse on Wyoming's state quarter show the state's history. The quarter came out in 2007.

Glossary

cowboy (KOW-boi): A cowboy is a man who takes care of cattle or horses. A cowboy appears on Wyoming's state quarter.

geysers (GUY-zurz): Geysers are springs that spray up hot water from holes in the ground. Geysers are in Wyoming's Yellowstone National Park.

mammal (MAM-ul): A mammal is a warm-blooded animal that has a backbone and hair; female mammals can produce milk to feed their babies. The bison is Wyoming's state mammal.

military (MIL-uh-tayr-ee): The military is the armed forces of a country. Fort Laramie was a military fort in Wyoming.

monument (MON-yuh-munt): A monument is an object that honors a person or an event. Devils Tower is a national monument in Wyoming.

museums (myoo-ZEE-umz): Museums are places where people go to see art, history, or science displays. Some people visit museums in Wyoming.

petals (PET-ulz): Petals are the colorful parts of flowers. The Indian paintbrush, Wyoming's state flower, has small red petals.

plains (PLAYNZ): Plains are areas of flat land that do not have many trees. Wyoming has plains.

popular (POP-yuh-lur): To be popular is to be enjoyed by many people. Hunting and fishing are popular in Wyoming.

ranches (RANCH-ez): Ranches are large farms for raising cattle or other large animals. Wyoming has many ranches.

seal (SEEL): A seal is a symbol a state uses for government business. Wyoming's seal shows a woman who stands for equal rights.

symbols (SIM-bulz): Symbols are pictures or things that stand for something else. The seal and the flag are Wyoming's symbols.

tourism (TOOR-ih-zum): Tourism is visiting another place (such as a state or country) for fun or the jobs that help these visitors. Tourism is popular in Wyoming.

Further Information

Books

Gagliano, Eugene. *C is for Cowboy: A Wyoming Alphabet*. Chelsea, MI: Sleeping Bear Press, 2003.

Keller, Laurie. *The Scrambled States of America*. New York: Henry Holt, 2002.

Thornton, Brian. *The Everything Kids' States Book: Wind Your Way Across Our Great Nation*. Avon, MA: Adams Media, 2007.

Web Sites

Visit our Web site for links about Wyoming: *childsworld.com/links*

Note to Parents, Teachers, and Librarians: We routinely verify our Web links to make sure they are safe and active sites. So encourage your readers to check them out!

Index